My Poisoned Perceptions

Janah Rima

BookLeaf Publishing

Presentation by *BookLeaf Publishing*

Web: www.bookleafpub.com

E-mail: info@bookleafpub.com

ISBN: 978-93-95784-16-0

First edition 2022

DEDICATION

To my big brother, thank you for allowing me to share and learn from you the art of literature and developing the emotional intelligence required to power through.

ACKNOWLEDGEMENT

Writing inspired by the beauty of nature, where the sky is a canvas and where roses hold magic.

PREFACE

Join me as we go on a journey, a pathway to growth and self-reflection. My Poisoned Perceptions is a glimpse of my view on life experiences and how they have shaped me. I look forward to sharing these experiences with you

Reflection

Sitting down alone one night.
I look up to see a face so bright.
A picture of innocence and wonderous looks,
A picture that can't be explained in a thousand books,
Sitting alone, I study her face,
A little button nose and ribbon of lace,
Her bottom lip slightly drawn in,
Just above her double chin,
Big, brown eyes that want to cry,
Maybe 'cause she's a little shy.
She's thinking thoughts that noone will know,
Like a secret little kingdom of music and art,
Her own little kingdom inside her heart.
I wish I could tell her it won't stay untouched,
That sometimes dreams can be easily crushed.
Indeed, all I do is watch the waves at sea,
Because I can't say a word as I'm looking at me.

Insecurities

A major role in the lives of many
We glance at our reflection
Flaws, we notice plenty
Clouding our thoughts
Negative judgement
Our souls, distraught
Unnecessary torment
Find comfort and implement
Self love and acceptance
Avoid the detriment
To your own transcendence

Self-Confidence

Whatever happened to your self-confidence?
You don't even display any sign of incompetence
Why do you constantly want to compare?
You feel as though you have flaws to repair
You fail to realise that they make you unique
For some reason all you want to do is critique
Ignore the social media stereotypes
You will never be of the same weight and height
What you see online is far from the truth
It's unfortunately slowly corrupting our youth
Shape your views based on the beauty that exists in the real world
Surely whatever you perceive online will leave your mind disturbed
Ever heard of the saying,
"We are all beautiful in our own way"
This differs from the message that social media tries to convey
But the change begins with you today
Confidence?
If you focus on yours,
You could have a positive impact on his and hers
Learn to love your unique qualities
For you owe no apologies

Simply because you are different
But my dear you are truly magnificent
So let's make a change, before positivity is
completely deceased
Even Beauty looked past the darkness in the
Beast

New Beginnings

She's always craved a fresh start
Somebody new to hold her heart
To turn over a new leaf
To rid her soul from all it's grief

"Take my hand and stroll with me
Into the horizon, there's alot to see"
New experiences, no more baggage
Happiness. To her,
Is a new language...

Rainy Days

Pitter-Patter
On a glass pane
Pitter-Patter
It's only rain

Often associated with gloom.
Though it's beauty,
Is far from doom.

Pitter-patter
Like steps of an infant
So precious and peaceful,
Appreciate it while silent

Soothing serenity
It's pure tranquility
Pitter-patter
This is divinity

Oath.

Reflect on what used to be
Shed some light on what is yet to come
Recognise the distance and you will see
All that hurt and made you numb

Our experiences shape our future self
Without them we are incapable of growth
Close the book, keep a stack on the shelf
I promise to keep my sanity

Catching Sunsets

Catching sunsets
Often makes me crave a reset
Praying we never met

All the lonely nights I spent
Wondering where you went
You left me alone,
But not really,
I'm at war with my thoughts.

Invasion…

An invasion like no other.
My thoughts take hold of my emotions.

Moving on was painful.
But how else would I have become the best
version of myself?

The sun may have set,
But its beauty will long remain.
When it rises, I hope to catch it...
With or without you.

~ O.R & J.R

Chasing Sunsets

Gone with the wind,
They all say.
As we reach the end,
Of yet another day.
Trembling hearts,
Hurtful cries.
Torn apart,
Painful sighs.

Chasing sunsets,
My friend so dear,
Is truly worth it,
For the end is near.

Shadows of the Rainbow

Shadows of the rainbow
"You reap what you sow"
Coloured emotion
Indirect communication

Love and devotion,
Anger and commotion,
Contradicting, it is so
Red is that colour of the rainbow

Sunshine and happiness,
No other way to express,
Feeling quite mellow?
Darling this is yellow.

Sadness and grief,
Just some old belief,
Questioning, nothing new,
"Honey, why are you feeling Blue?"

Sure, there are many more, but keep an open mind, my fellow readers, for are these not the base colours by which the rest stem from?

Now these may be stereotypical associations,
But this is just social appropriation
Look deep into the shadows of the rainbow
Precious soul, “you reap what you sow”

Strategy

My darling love,
With you,
My heart, I entrust
•
Incapable of love,
Foolish boy,
This is lust
•
I love you,
All truth,
Not a word of a lie
•
False truths,
I'm afraid,
You're awaiting my demise
•
You and I
Unite in love
•
Foolish boy,
I'm calling your bluff.

Dark Night

You see that's the thing with demons...
They eat at you in the darkest hour of night
For no other reason than to fill your soul with
fright.
My dearest baby as you lay here,
Your broken soul filled with fear
Your precious heart trembling with every tear...
Will you really allow them to cause you fear?
Will you let them invade your mind,
And let them use what they find,
To shape how you really feel inside?

Tiktok

The sound of silence holds terror.
Piercing screams shattering mirrors.
Trust.
A regretful error.
Clock is ticking.
The horror.
Is it over?
Or are we forever?

Love or lust?

She allows him to consume her mind,
But he wishes for her body.
She's aware that love can be blind,
And it's more than just a hobby.

Love? A word so underestimated and overused.
Do we really know the extents of the term?
I doubt it. It's been deeply abused.
We use it lightly, while our hearts crash and burn.

Differentiate between love and lust.
Love is a connection,
You'll develop a sense of trust.
Lust is mere attraction,
Temporary satisfaction.

Home

"Let's move away"
Saying it with such ease and no delay
All I want is just to stay
Here at home where everything is okay
I know that's not the ideal way
But change has never been a favourable game to play
Home is where I hope to return at the end of each day
In my mind it isn't so far away
I can't comprehend how you could ask me to stray
From my safe place, I really need to stay
"We're moving away"
Your statement has changed
All of a sudden my world has turned grey
Are you really going to drag me away
It is here where my heart wishes to stay
I raise my hands and I pray
That you agree and here we remain
But all I hear is "don't complain"
You're adamant on leaving, but here, I will stay
I know if we go,
The clouds will roll in,
And may they begin, my gloomy days

Modern Love

He thinks of her,
Sex appeal.
He consumes her mind,
She thinks it's real.
Only referring to her as "baby",
But she asks about the future,
His response is "maybe".
Could this be love?
She can't possibly comprehend.
He wears her like a glove,
And in public, "she's just a friend."
His intentions are far from pure,
Falling into his trap, she was blind.
How he felt about her. He was unsure.
Her true love. She is yet to find.

Confusion

Confusion.
Is this real or are you a mere illusion?
They warn me to avoid the delusion
I can't live a life of exclusion
I apologise for any intrusion
But my darling this relies on inclusion
Love isn't based on a revolution
It's working to find a solution
We're both expected to place a contribution
But you have me lost in this world of confusion
Battling with the idea of substitution
For this really is no solution
To the problem which has no conclusion
So tell me please,
How do I deal with such confusion?

Psychology

Let's have a chat about mental health
A concept that is definitely more important than your wealth
We tend to ignore this essential aspect
Because of this, there's a longer-lasting effect
Negativity begins to cloud your judgement
Constantly placing yourself in unwanted predicaments
Disregarding your peace of mind
Leads people to constantly question "are you doing fine?"
We brush aside our mental health
Or simply just stack it up on the shelf
Thinking it'll be able to stand alone
But it gets to a point where our life problems are overblown
We shouldn't allow this to overwhelm us
Instead we should clean the shelf from it's dust
Give our mental state a chance to breathe
Place it in an atmosphere with a cool and steady breeze
Clear your state of mind from negative thoughts
Fill it with motivation and avoid being distraught
Mental health, not a simple concept

But it's one we should definitely accept
It's fundamental in order to grow
To focus on psychology
Before it's too late
And you owe yourself an apology…

Intoxicated

A sip of wine
Shattered glass
You were mine.
My greatest loss

Wilted rose
Broken hearts
Rivers flow
We’re torn apart

Thoughts mystified
Vertigo.
You’re terrified
Darling, I know

Graceful strokes
Upon my skin.
Oak.
Royalty, feels like sin.

Fantasy

He introduced her to the wild side.
He was that bit of excitement on a summer day.
He was the light that shone and lit up the whole street.
He was the wave that washed up against the shore and took a piece of her back every time.
He was the glimpse of hope to a better life.
He was her safe place.

He was...
a memory of her imagination.
A fantasy...
That which did not exist.

She realised, she was all of that and more.
She found it within her soul.
She thanks him for that.
For although he is a product of her creative mind,
He contributed to her journey in finding herself.

Missed Opportunities

I waited patiently for you to arrive.
Every knock on the door,
I ran, praying it was you.
Constantly disappointed,
When will you come through?

Enduring the prolonged wait,
I'm keen to know what you have for me
You've given everybody a chance,
But I have not yet met you.
When will you make your appearance?

I have greeted many,
But none of them were you.
I was after something specific,
But it was getting hard to maintain my
optimism.

My doubts are swarming in,
When will my turn come?
You're taking your sweet time.

My patience has worn thin.

Wait...

A knock on my door.
Have you finally arrived?

Nope. Again. Not you.
I took a step back.

Reality...
All this time, I didn't know.
You were waiting at my door.
It was you all along,
Greeting me in various forms.
You weren't neglecting me,
I was just blind, and ignored the signs
But you, my friend,
Were opportunity in disguise...

Fire and Ice

I am a mixture of fire and ice...
Your innocent mind may question what I mean,
as these are two completely different elements
on opposite sides of the spectrum.

Fire refere to the fierce yet warm heart that
resides within me. My soul is pure but it's firm
when need be.

Ice signifies how cold I can be towards those
who have hurt me. I grow a strong ice wall
around my ribcage to stop the warmth of my
heart from being exposed to the wrong people.

You may think it's odd to have ice as a barrier
from fire coming out. But you see in this broad
imagination of mine, if the fire melts the ice, the
ice becomes water, and what puts out the fire?

www.ingramcontent.com/pod-product-compliance
Lightning Source LLC
Chambersburg PA
CBHW051754130826
49812CB00033B/1153
* 9 7 8 9 3 9 5 7 8 4 1 6 0 *